To Jeff
You have great
talent & potential.

8/3/2013

Selected Poems and Passions: 2004 – 2011

William F. DeVault

edited by M.K. Brake

Other books by William F. DeVault include

PanthEon	ISBN #0-9659576-0-8
From an Unexpected Quarter	ISBN #0-5950023-1-5
Love Gods of a Forgotten Religion	ISBN #0-5952225-2-8
101 Great Love Poems (Hardbound)	ISBN #0-5956540-2-9
101 Great Love Poems (Softbound)	ISBN #0-5952588-2-4
INVOCATO	ISBN #1-4116293-1-0
THE COMPLEAT PANTHER CYCLES	ISBN #1-4116379-4-1
The Morgantown Suite Poems	ISBN #1-4116337-4-1
Ronin in the Temple of Aphrodite	ISBN #978-1-4303-0425-8
Psalms of the Monster River Cult	ISBN #978-1-4357-0728-3
(co-authored with Daniel S. McTaggart)	
As such…	ISBN #978-1-4357-1448-9
loveaddict	ISBN #978-0-557-28390-3
Selected Poems and Passions: 2004-2011	ISBN #978-0-615-54937-8

Selected Poems and Passions: 1996-2004
© William F. DeVault

Published by Apokalypsis
ISBN:1478176768

www.cityoflegends.com
ISBN #978-1-478-17676-3

To those who dare to love and dream

The notion of doing a book of this era's poetry seems odd to me. So much of my life from the mid-late 90's is insane and highly public. But, the truth is, some good poetry came in those furnaces, some of my best.

So, here it is, from my divorce and exile to Los Angeles to the end of my second marriage, these are some of the works that saved my life and found their way to literary journals and across the internet. From the Panther Cycles to "Damascus", from Pink Jade to "from out of the city".

Some pretty raw stuff. Raw in the sense of true and natural and pure.

When this era began I had not even met the woman who was going to become the Leopard and my second (ex-)wife. I was incredibly naïve about many things, but I learned, I toughened, I grew. And I wrote. I wrote a lot. By the end of it I was divorced from the Leopard and had spent an almost-futile exile year in Mississippi, and had written some superior works in my catalog.

So, to Jan and Lauri, Karla and Robin, Dar and Ann, Jasmin and Kristina, and so many others; some who inspired volumes in their own rights, some who are merely a line or a subtext to a thought here and there; some midwifed my dreams, others crept into the nursery, knife and bag of serpents in hand, meaning harm and havoc, I thank you all. I am grateful.

I am also grateful for the support and aid of both M.K. Brake and Mariya Andriichuk, who both played pivotal roles in this volume.

William F. DeVault
April 28, 2013

i

Table of Contents

Aureate

I will not find what I am looking for
here amoung the shadowdancers and sunbathers.
hearts aureate swim to the horizons, or climb cliffs
to seek their destinies in moments frozen as they arc their
breathless forms out and away
from the rocks of despair, to slice the air
in a dart that acknowledges life is best
tasted at terminal velocity,
striking the glass sea that mirrors not for long
the double speed descent
as hopeful and hopeless romantics dare to live and love
and share and dream and fly and fall and rise and bend and rule
a domain of the senses. seven,

at my last count. mounting the
sandstone pedestals
left by the spittle of God against the eroding sanctuaries
of our immutable malleability.
and when we break the surface tension of our own pretensions,
we ride the shockwaves like perilous nightmares
to the foothills of the precipice,
practicing the perfecting pain that shall stain our legacies,
whether we hide from it or not, caught on ourselves to coin
effigies in words that make mockery of the currency of our barter.
seven sins forgiven. the eighth

breaking the seal of blissful arrogance.
and the water slips past your form
as your momentum conquers the
buoyancy of swimmers in the sea of life
and the force of your entry takes you deep.
past where the children sleep. into the depths
where the sun of forced gaiety does not penetrate.
towards the oblivion of knowledge.

the tree of life is a seaweed now, a fruit that floats on limbs
thin with the wear of age and memory.
and with every dive, a little closer to fingers split and bloody
with the violence of the splitting of the aqueous walls
seen only as a looking glass by those for whom life is
too deep to fathom, too dark to see, too cold to warm, too true to trust.

city of angels

lost soul.
a city of lights of stimulated
noble gases. it passes
for a faux firmament.
I haven't seen an angel
here.
and probably,
never will.

but I have seen
poor, proud people,
their flannel workshirts
needing repair and a wash,
shuffling through the
immigrant neighborhoods.
the pretty girl, pretty no more,
selling her star power
in condom come-ons
on the street corner.
and I have seen a peaceful
ocean, kissing the sands
of time, worn like
strands of beige pearls
on the neck of a lady too
proud to admit the paste
will wash away in the rain.

love is bought here. sold
in carrying cases with
rouge and eyeliner. t-shirts
filled with silicone brush
the vanity from the wind
as rollerblades run down
bag ladies who never
gave that producer the
blowjob he asked for.

war zone. everyone
sells something. fortunately,
I am wise enough, and studied
well enough in the wars of the
sphere of Venus, I know I have
nothing of any real value.
which makes me the richest man
in the city of angels. until
I give out, give up, give in
to the inevitable.

the curve of parallel lines

complacency breeds the lowest of lives,
edges dulled until they reflect only the memory of sharpness,
the arch recollections of past positions and penetrations.
souls sold into an elegant enslavement as we circumvent
the radii of our oblong hearts.
start from the top and trace me a pattern, born cold,
worn old in the furrows of brows knit with thrice told yarns,
kisses that dangle at the angle between melody and harmony,
the tunes told in triumph and transcendence and tempests
that washed us to the quick them sent us on our way to play
a game of mumble the peg, a tune of soundless atonality.
kodo drums driving us out into the night. light passing
for heat, heat passing for fire, fire passing for passion.
and all through the night we keep watch on the clocksprings
as they wind. inexorably. down to the last frail turns.

fireflowers

I could learn to live amoung the fire flowers,
at least for a season at a time. Crime of passion,
sins of commission, omission and emission burning
their molten silver trails across tongues hungry
for a taste of the dark communion of lovers
and friends, blending desire with the will of children
breaking their covenants at will in random
captures of elusive emotions and experiences shared,
dared and bared within small corridors to be kept sealed
by the hearts that dare walk them against the tapestries
we would burn rather than show to the face of the crowds.

Santa Ana winds

Like a wave of fire descending in judgement.
Burning me to the quick.
Thick with self-denial,
the trial of the Romantique.
Seeking truth
in the shallows of the rain forest,
poorest of the depths.
Having slept with the demons,
awakened to the silence
and foresworn the violence
in the best Buddheo-Christian traditions
made proof of the truth of a lie accepted with a smile,
while
all the while
knowing that in a medicated haze,
all praise is lies.

Pray for the wind.

Pray it will not be defiled by
this child of my blackened heart,
that my final torment will not be as epic
as the tragedy of false hopes,
fed the bread bought at Borders.
Filling chalices
with the urine of mad marketers
made rich on pain gained at the cost of the children.
And I
will ride the winds,
even if the only vector left is
down.
Down to the foot of the cliffs of the legends.

Pray for the wind.

TRANSCENDENCE

the heavens are in heat tonight
for this penitent, penetrative dream.

the iron lion stands astride memory.
mantichore wings of black lace fragments
of a leather lost to the weather of whim.
to him alone is there an accounting.

countdown.

grey skies to brown toxic fumes
as the hypergolic moments when
soul and intellect touch in the ceramic chamber
of a nautilus heart.

the skies scream aside in a fictional friction
of breath drawn out to thread like taffy
pulled too long.
an obit of an orbit, undecayed
as the patina colossus pulls free his lame heel
from the grounding earth
and raises high the last romantic verb.

liftoff.

and I am gone.
gone beyond imagination.
a consecration of madness
sold in gold and honeysuckle silver.
quicksilver slowed to sublimate
into a crystalline matrix of time.

farewell.
farewell.

but it is no longer my concern.
for I burn tonight in orbit no longer.
stronger than an epiphany
made construct in the shallows of an id.

angels sleep

angels sleep a shift when we repose,
knowing that life goes on and that even sentinels
must nod from time to time.
and, knowing that I am safe in your arms,
and you in mine,
they need not watch every moment.

I saw you dance, unconsciously, listening
to Ani DiFranco sing about leaving in the morning
and the futility of shyness
when the clock runs short, like a dead end road
between the towers of downtown Los Angeles.

so, ride with me if you dare
ride with me if you care
ride with me, and your hair
will shine with the jewels you tossed
in small hand across the open fields
when you stopped to contemplate three wishes
already well on their way to being granted,
by being planted in my garden.

autumnal memory

the smell of burning leaves
always reminds me of my father.
a good man. honest and kind.
all my girlfriends who ever met him
fell in love with him.
but I saw him first.

a touch of Heather

And tonight
a young woman
on the cusp of the silence of yesterday
and the variations of tears and joy to come
will read a dog eared copy of her favourite poet
and he will touch her.

Six thousand miles
from where he wrote the words
and three thousand miles from where he lived them
at the time of their emergence from the stream of thought
into ink to press to paper like lips against flesh.
And they will touch her.

The lights flee
to the touch of the nun marking curfew
and she is left with the pale blue curve of moonlight
as she draws the last syllables across her tongue
like the prayer she recited for her teachers this morning.
And they will touch her.

Eyes to mind.
Mind to heart. Heart to hands that play stand in
for a man she'll never meet face to face, flesh to flesh.
But her hands play second to his absence and she learns,
lessons caught in fingertip expressions of borrowed ardour.
And they touch her.

The night reigns.
And she is lost in the exploration of darkness
that draws her from this place, grey walls on the green land.
Her ragged, hot breaths, played out for an abstract lover
on an island touched not by his feet or hands or eyes.
And he touches her.

Glass roses

conceive of a flower.
like no other.
no colour,
but the curving clarity,
the photic charity
of crystalline silence.
past the rainbow's violence.
a white fragrance,
white as a virgin's first kiss,
or the lost heartbeat I gave over
to the universe when
first we met,
when first I set my sails
for a new horizon,
passion and pride put down
and sacrificed
to the gods of love.
to the holders of dreams.
to the bearers of my gift.
to wings that take their lift
from the winds of sorrow.
a meadow of perfect blossoms
refracting the light you give me
onto a page of history and hope.
my brother, the night, takes me,
and I am not tomorrow anymore.
but my words endure.
pure
as a field of glass roses.
row upon perfect chaotic row
not discovered in this incarnation.
but they are out there.

brisant revelations

expect the apocalypse
if a vow as sacred as I have taken
should prove
mutable in the wills
and winds
and currents of the human heart,
stolen from the fires of a Promethian glory
unshackled to the punishing stone
to atone for the arrogance of hope
and love
and empowering the juggernaut.
actions refracted in colours of a spectrum
that runs not from red to violet
but from osmium to radium
through silver and platinum and gold and rhodium
polished to a rosary of alpha particles
striking ghostly glowing receptors
in a flint and steel approach to making
nuclear fusion of lovers' sweat.
breaking down the waters
to make hydrogen and oxygen,
breathing in the latter
and fusing the former
in a thermonuclear glory
that rises like the sun in a heart
finally released like Glatisant
to stalk the legends of a lost mythology.
where the Gods walk only in tandem.
as it should be.

the patchwork skirt of my love

the sound of soft fingertips across the strings of a lute.
strumming the memories. humming the melody of life.
and I am lost in the possibilities of your presence,
pleasant, peasant prayers that lead to the summit
of the mountain in the distance, where legends reign.

kings cannot know this brandywine. princes pass perplexed.
and all the bishops seem ignorant of the nature of God
when their ignorance of the crux of creation is displayed,
paraded in the sudden dance of a smiling child by the fire.
and I am lost in the reverent reveries of this revelation.

play for me that melody, the one you tried to teach me,
you tried to reach me with when I despaired of lost love
and the angels and faeries all seemed annoying pinpoints
that pricked and sticked and stole the moment that was mine
and you came for me, barefoot and arrogant, like a poet.

and the fires swam into the sky and I, I was reborn.
torn to pieces and re-assembled like a patchwork skirt
to brush your bare legs in the summer heat and to defeat
the angry winds that would come down from the mountains,
mounting the horses of hoarfrost to charge your charms.

I live now, in more than just abstract recollections of a score
of forgetful lovers who would not give me second thought
were it not for the trinkets of my words they wear as bright badges
as they tell their tales of the pale blue moon of memory.
and they don't wear the patchwork skirt of my love. or play the lute.

William F. DeVault

close your eyes

close your eyes
that you do not see the walls dissolve
beneath the silent tears I shed
as I reach out and brush trembling lips
with trembling lips
that seek to speak a truth I have not words
well made enough to communicate.
but can speak with touch so eloquently.
if you will but close your eyes.

I rained poetry

there is no fear on the edge:
joy.

joy is what I find in the instants
between moments
when my feet are touching nothing but
sky
and the rocks recede
to return.
sooner or later.
driven by grave gravity
and the intemperate nature of natural law.
but
in the brisant moment,
leaping from
precipice to precipice,
I am reborn,
triggered and transfigured.

worn away are the chains of
the pains of
the stains of
mortal mediocrity
and I -
I am one with the clouds.

and I rain poetry.
(for that is my nature.)

as you turn your face skyward
to catch a few drops
on a tongue parched
by the dry air of memory
and the sun of shallow sentiments,
sold in the Hallmark rack
in the name of mass seduction.

and I rain poetry.

to irrigate the fields of forever
and make them ready for the seeds
planted without your realizing it
when you waved to me
as I ran the cliffs
high above the plains of stale acceptance.
and danced.
and danced.
and danced like a hurricane.
at the thought of you,
naked in the rain.

and I rained poetry.

bringing the thunder at the appropriate moment
when all other senses were spent
and only sound could
penetrate

the wet shell of overloaded synapses.
what passes for the echo
of fire that surged
and purged
the very ions of our irony.

and I rained poetry.

calling the winds to lift me.
to gift me with the words
that you would carry,
eroded into your sandstone soul.
nevermore the monolith,
but an aggregate of your essence
with flecks of my pitchblende.
bound to you by eloquence
that quenched an ancient thirst,
cursed to you
in a garden you will never see
except in the mirages of the maelstrom.

and I rained poetry.

and it was nothing.
compared to a single, honest kiss.
but it was,
in the absence of passion,
a worthy golem in the armies of solitude
up
on the cliffs
where I still dance with the winds.
and call the thunder.
even when no one watches.
or cares
or dares
to dance along.
(for that is my nature.)

the ancient brain

your sheen of sweat
whets my appetites
for the nights of incoherent light
merging into new colours.
hold tight to all my angles
and I will intersect
memories you did not know you were capable of
but dimly saw in a fantasy rendered
in colors of solferino and pale blue.
sound for me that song again,
the one with only rhythm and words
that work only in the context
of satin and silk and scents that went
straight to the ancient brain.

tip for tap

tip for tap. the crush and thrust of contact made,
displayed, paraded in a prayed-for instinct of distinction.

run red, the heart is bled.
run red, the heart is bled.
and all that I have said
is to get you into bed.

chaste chasings on the framework of folly, ornate
to innate feelings. irate thought censors sent packing.

run red, the heart is bled.
run red, the heart is bled.
and all my passions, dead,
awake to mourners, fled.

crimson lips to solferino folds, gold to the barter,
the starter's pistol for my heart discharges rainbows.

run red, the heart is bled.
run red. the heart is bled.
and these thoughts are all wed
by a weaving of romantique's thread.

tip for tap, the crush and thrust of contact made,
displayed, paraded in a prayed for instinct of distinction.

radiant tigers

welcome to the land of radiant tigers.
bright eyes like coherent beaming ruby rods
fiercely piercing the fearjungle of life.
pouncing like Lord Byron on a first draft.

poets glide on the slip and slide emotions
whetted and wet with the potions of passion.
sweetmeats met in a feast of least persistence,
an insistence on the order of a random universe.

roadwork with the soda jerk mixology of words
that effervesce with a laugh in the daft draught
of expressions caught caterwauling to glance
off the silvered glass mirrors of albedo'd radiance.

welcome to the land of radiant tigers.
citrus stripes on cocoa black, warm as memory.
cold as calculations in an impatient ledger,
counting found funds, lost time, and three deep breaths.

TEMPEST

Take into your palm the merest scent of the rain
the taste of the clouds brought down to fill the sculpted rims
of earth laid open to catch the essence of life.
Grounded, pounded flat by the cold courage of ages past,
at last we find the run of the water makes meanders of our hearts.
Rivers of our souls.
Lakes of our illusions.
Oceans of our desperations
to sail upon when we are stale within our failing lives.
Knives honed on the waterglass of our saline runoff.
Kissing the idols of our Poseidons
from which rise our Aphrodites.
Which touch the clouds with their beauty
and bring the tears to wet again the sterile ground.
And we wait for the thundergods
to bring the storm. Hot on the heels of the cooling clouds
that weep upon as they reap from us our thankfulness.
And the lightning never fails to elicit
a sudden twinge of terror.
As the thunder rolls
and our souls fold in upon themselves in mirror mockery
of the opening leaves that drink the tempest's tears
and give us a taste of ambrosia.

Dare we cross the Rubicon?

dare we cross the Rubicon
that lays behind your door?
where sheets and skin and perfumed sin
shall draw us from the floor?
topple our frail dignities
of manners and restraint.
proves to us this fiery rush
is no false suitor's feint?

would you dare to see my scars
that run beneath the veil?
would you dare release your dreams
and climb, where others fail
to hold their breath until their death
is crescent to their prayers?
both barefoot and bare headed, bold,
to climb celestial stairs.

where heaven waits behind the gates
and passion is the key.
where wanting all is not the fall
if you trust your destiny.
dare we cross the Rubicon
that lays behind your door?
where sheets and skin and perfumed sin
shall call us, evermore.

how would you have me touch you?

how would you have me touch you?
how soon? how oft? how soft?
would you have me lay back on the bed
and let you rise, aloft?

would you ask I play seduction
so that you can play ingenue?
or would you like to take the lead
and teach me a thing or two?

shall I wine and dine and sweep you
off you feet and on your back?
or shall this be a blue jeans thing
or a tryst of a darker tack?

may it be to your great pleasure
if I insist your essence kissed,
that I may wait to penetrate
until you have found your bliss?

and would you let me hold you
for the night, or for a while,
and feel the heat between us
and taste the comfort of my smile?

how would you have me touch you?
how soon? how oft? how soft?
would you have me lay back on the bed
and let you rise, aloft?

TITAN

water to earth
earth to air
air to fire
to be quenched by the waves

nobody saves anybody
in the end
my friend
it all ends badly
sadly
for the brave soldiers
on the barricades
playing charades
of national anthems
and a battlecry
that will die
soon after the sound

pounding the walls
of stone and earth
with fists made bloody
by the ruddy soil
boiling away the clay
to leave us
something primal
criminal
and best forgotten
a test gone rotten
and the eggs float
like a capsized boat
unable to carry anything
but an object lesson

the riddle of impatience

warmth enough for two,
few share with any sense of synergistic sin,
but take skin between tender talons and test
the winds of surrender to the forces of a sky
red rimmed and rapacious, the cursed thirst
drawing out of us the need to bleed seed
in the consecration of the warm wine,
christening the glistening membranes
with pain and stain and swain's refrain,
learned in the cunning craft of seductions.
and we are not better than the bettors
who lost their nerve and took short odds
rather than seek the skies on the way to heaven
in and through the arms and charms of love.

Jasmine and Plumeria

I will
pass my heat
through oils and essences
held in my hand
just long enough to
pass my heat
into your skin.
your soft
fragrant
skin.
every pore
every curve
every nerve
begging touch
like a child
seeking reassurance.
and as I
pass my heat
into you, the alchemy
begins and the thin skin
turns oil
into gold
that you hold,
every fold,
every plain and ridge
and tensing membrane
calling my name
in silent
invocation
celebration
consecration.
as I dare
pass my heat
into your fires.

The taste of remembrance

you reminded me of memory.
not a memory.
but memory.

that twisted lift of something.
something. something caught
on the roof of my mouth
like peanut butter.

but it is a soft mystery
that wafted in on winds
I had not smelled
since midnight in Venice,
with the jasmine
and the dreams
that coiled in eddies of air
caught in the shadows
that melted into you.

true to your nature.
true to my hunger.

your shoulders bare to my touch.
your eyes closed to my thoughts.
and all else open and warm
and something like music.
something like music
when it comes upon you
suddenly, but beautifully,
like a lover at first waking.

and memory tasted a lot
like your lips.

the frost of ill-remembranced things

sacred whims, foresworn this night,
we banked them in the dark
to hide from sight a blessed light
in which we shield our mark.

a print that hands and solemn bands
can not and never steal.
a kiss, amiss, and yet in bliss,
to, by this choosing, seal.

in autumn I did drop my plumes
and slowed to sullen pace,
and barely made the sheltered rooms
to sleep a winter's brace.

and comes the spring on powdered wing
to wake me from my grave,
to test the mettle of this thing
we fought and sought to save.

votive

the cycle cuts both ways
and the haze that lays upon the sky
falls in cascades unafraid of your perceptions.
conceptions, missed and made, kissed and played
for a fool, held in continuous catalepsies.

the promise makes a mark.
stark realizations evoking amotations
in the mouths of children reaching for the golden apples,
sold and consumed in fists fitful and frail.
the sail of the horizon turns away, if only in the dimlight.

the riddle takes it's toll.
soul food for the role we all play in the dance.
chances exchanged in dances made to execute a single turn.
and we burn. oh we burn with incandescent passions,
fashioned in the image of our gods, however we build them.

the memory remains to tell.
and we will share it when we dare again to feel something
less than the most that we toast our fall over, the wine
of wisdom running across tongues made numb with the spices
that twice as oft as not have burnt our lips for a draught of heaven.

the Nosferatu's quandary

The night grows long, the hunger deep,
I can feel it in me, as I sleep,
a hollow womb of poisoned thought
that floods with passions scattershot.
That I might rise to walk the trail
where lovers strive and lovers fail
will not be left to destiny,
castoff, aloft, to plummet free
and gather speed and gather seed
and, in the end, to gather need
to blight the night with crippling pain
until I dare to feed again.

the taste of a shy smile

sliding by
the sky
we touch on
several planes
in wavelengths
beyond violet and red
the past is dead
and serves
the purpose
of conduit
to deliver
us
to this moment
suspended
between what was
and what is possible
which is
everything
yet to be explored
not ignored
like opportunities
for joy
by cold and craven players
in fading photographs
and memories

I know things
that toe rings
and a hint of jasmine
can't communicate
fate and hate
are not sibling or regent
and we prevent
our own happiness
in cowardice
and a curious logic
that begs the tragic
refusal to love

because we know we are
unworthy
but that doesn't stop God
or poets
and the taste
of a shy smile
should be immortal

the philosophy of dreams

touch me. for I am flesh, as you,
given to the same needs for air and food
and warmth, communicated between two bodies
at rest, touching in all aspects possible.
and many improbable,
as I pull a cat out of the quantum corner
and make it into roses to bloom in arcs
of every colour of a spectrum of another sphere
as they fill the room with exotic perfumes
I brought back with me on a trip to the stars.

sing for me. I will smile and touch your hair
and dare to sing along, when I know the words.
for we are at best in blended voice and thought
and flesh, yes, I recall mere moments ago
when I could not tell the terminus between
your light and my darkness, as angels averted eyes
and we made the case for unity between us.
it was. yes, it was. it was something I will write of
when I catch my breath and I can find words unique
and perfect and passionate enough.

dream of me. for I dream of you. I dreamt of you
even before I heard your voice. before I knew your name.
when all I knew was that, by the same evidence that I know
that there is a God, you exist and existed and I would find you,
even if I had to climb mountains of madness and sail,
sail forever, it seemed, on seas of the mediocrity of life.
for there is too much to be lost to the world if I was right.
if love is and was and will be regent. regret wets sweated sins.
but I am a penitent pilgrim, lost on the road to Golgotha.
seeking something more than the philosophy of dreams.

and I will sleep alone

I will sleep tonight and dream dreams
I cannot express until new words
are forged in the heart of the world.
Words bright and black and so fresh and hot
they burn the skin of the hands that hold them,
but are as soothing as lemon ice on a parched tongue.

And I will sleep
alone.
Not by choice, but by design,
as the sailor on a sea of memory
seeks new horizons,
but for all his skill and talent
must make do with the wind that comes.

Deep and hungry pockets

I am lost.
lost to the light, to the night.
white on white is my banner of war,
boring plainsong to a tuneless drumming,
humming like an indifferent hive
of stingless bees, high in the trees
above the patient earth,
worth little when the honey runs dry.
and I
need to pull the knife out of my back
and get a life where my knack
for giving more than I get
is welcomed with more than
deep and hungry pockets.
all used up
and the cup is less than half full now.
a vow of unbent knees
so close to being broken,
unspoken is the sixth word,
but it was heard before.
when the floor was wood
and life was good
and love was not an obscenity.
an amenity
to be bartered off
to be placed
in deep and hungry pockets.

the poisoned pen

The troubadour, he knows the truth, unsuspected and unspoken,
that tears the soul of every man whose heart and mind lay broken:
Dreamers die, for a poet's lie, at peace with their transgressions.

The miller and the blacksmith are at peace with their professions,
the priest will carry on his trade and take the strange confessions.
The troubadour, he knows the truth, unsuspected and unspoken.

The sentry knows to challenge foes when in the night he's woken
from the disturbing thought born from what is in the barrels oaken:
Dreamers die, for a poet's lie, at peace with their transgressions.

The mistress and the novice seek each her own perfections.
The baker fires his ovens to be lost in his confections.
The troubadour, he knows the truth, unsuspected and unspoken.

Warriors die for causes both obscured and held as the slogan
of their leaders, prayers in the shadows of Holy vows now broken.
Dreamers die, for a poet's lie, at peace with their transgressions.

Take these words as a sign of faith and as my memory's token,
the realization stands apart, against all false impressions.
The troubadour, he knows the truth, unsuspected and unspoken:
Dreamers die, for a poet's lie, at peace with their transgressions.

Will you be with me tonight?

will you be with me tonight
when the demons come?
all the doubts running like molten wax
from the wick of my heart, trimmed
too tightly by anxious hands...
holding me against the lost causes
I sold out for you and your eyes,
spinning webs that I can never cut,
never tear, never touch for fear
that you might one day awaken
and realize that there is someone
in this world besides yourself.

flowers for your hair

if I gave you flowers for your hair
would you wear them? or would
you put them away in a vase somewhere
for future reference in case you could not find
better blossoms or a better suitor
to dance on the beach with?
and would you be strong enough,
to answer when asked,
where you got the flowers from,
when the jealous boys at the well asked
their fists clenched in
self-targeted cowardice? there are no
right answers to the riddle. but I have
little time for vases and evasions.
love is meant to be a simple thing
that we poison only with artifice
and our own shortcomings. wear
the flowers and dance with me
in the twilight, and I will everyday
find new flowers to add fragrance
to your life. to your love. to your heart.

ecstasy

The long, slow, inexorable slide into ecstasy,
subtle and not so silent that you cannot hear your doubts
as your own shouts drown out your blushing conscience.
Patience rewarded, hoarded passion tapped to flow undammed
like tears wept throughout our electric union.
Fire consecrating this sacrifice made to build upon
a question unasked but taken on the tip of a silver tongue
in silent worship of your flesh and your heart and your mind.

my life

My life. It is my life to make of it what I choose.
I will win, and lose
and smile more often than not.
Courage will give me hope. Hope will give me
strength. And strength
will give me the courage to seek new truths.

And I will never love without a sense
of wonder and awe at the
infinite possibilities within the human heart...
and the beauty of dreams, held iron and ironic
within even the most tragic
fall from grace and the dreams of the damned.

And I will not be given to despair, for I have stood
in fires I could not fathom
and held my breath until death seemed sibling
to the pain within my soul. For this experiment
of my life will have validity
within the scientific method of the universe.

A sky, wet with tears

part the skies with the sweet saline of tears of angels
watching with silent shame at our self-immolative madness.
pride that hides a thousand cowardices, the root of weakness,
we seek the bleak shallows of the desert rivers, a curse that tells
all there is to know about our paper hearts. spirits windblown
like the dandelion fluff and milkweed faeries that carry seed
too often into sterile earth, to wither amid the stones that feed
on our very impertinent apathy. free of remorse, pebbles sown
to litter the salted fields of a potter's grave, slave to error.
the village idiots of an age of electrons, speaking in child scrawl
on a tabula rasa for the deaf and the dumb that still hear the call
to arms to seek the fellowship of kindred hearts in a mirror.
clouds on wings as oft leathery as feathery, as bitter and black
as the wax of a candle snuffed with dry fingers holding nothing back.

Uriah

and for all these things, they are now but dust.
crushed beneath the heels of the celestial waterclock
that grinds us down with tears and tempestuous synapses.
seizing our days in slivers of life. the knife has no handle,
and thus we must rip our own flesh to fight the war
we promenade into like dancers in a royal spectacle.
mirrors bend the light and we might see something
of ourselves in the eyes of strangers called to kiss
the edge of our self-immolations...
but in the end, no one stands alone, or they fall.
and the walls of Jericho still mock the memory
of the stonemason.
for, in words, there are no truth.
but in our hearts.
in our hearts,
those cold orbs we cover over in varnished iconography
we flee to when we cannot deal with hope.
cold and kinetic like a snowball fight
on a dark December night.
white out.
right out of a prophecy
written with fingers still wet.
night sweat.
and a game of liar's poker
played to lose.
arrayed to lose
like Uriah at the wall.
left to die
for a purpose
he did not comprehend,
for he did not know
the currency of history.

laying down the tools of pain

We are better than our rationale, fashioning
our fronted personalities on lessons learned
and burned into us with the lash of pain, fading
only slightly in the shadows of our somnambulance.
I have lived more than a life in my life, and found
that the unilateral gift is better than the exchange
of poisoned arrows, narrow heart, narrow minds,
those who stand behind the pillars rather than atop,
and never taste the truth without a smirk. Yet, still,
life is more than the madness we perpetuate when we
close our minds, close our hearts, close our lives
to the infinite possibilities of love. And if I alone
understand this, I will not bend, will not pretend
that I can bury words and actions with a shrug, for
it is better to love alone than hate with the masses,
for when we let down the fears that drive us, we
achieve at least a shadow of the image of God.

Damascus, Movement 7

"Humble seulement en face de Dieu."
And so the great I Am must have loaned
a reasonable likeness to you.

For I am humbled. Cut down to size,
a bite size morsel for digestion
in the gullet of the phoenix.

The image of the Maker reborn
in graceful secrets, a sadness set
in stones of jet and jade and sapphire.

I have cut the stones we selected.
I have kissed the hems of the elected.
I have sheathed the souls, unprotected.

Wings drawn to launch pirouettes to land
amid dry stones and forgotten bones
left on the desert floor by the road.

Afterimages of shadowdance.
Bright shades casting calculated crimes
in stark relief of the honored dead.

"Humble seulement en face de Dieu."
So the prophecy and loss, counted
in killing stones, is crushed to the crust.

Sacraments in a cul de sac sent
skimming over the bleached beach sand dunes
that stretch far and away into hope.

I cast the runes in ridddles, rhythm'd
to force slow staccato memory
to telegraph the tempest tonight.

I will worship with my memories,
I will worship with my threnodies,
I will worship with my vanities.

Zeus and Apollo, Odin and Thor,
small gods of passion, small gods of war,
acolytes on acid etch the night.

Futility folds a hand of prayer
and draws, to an inside straight, a queen
to take the place of fours and knaves.

"Humble seulement en face de Dieu."
I will touch the face of God tonight,
and offer earnest prayers in the dark.

wine

touching softly the fringe of your hairline, testing the holy waters
of the sweat that forms on your brow, even when it is cool,
as the fool rushes not in this time, but begs the wine
of an earnest heart to age to full flavour and ripe with intoxication
made manifest in the last kiss I place on lips begging
to be crushed so that the juices may flow from the cask
and down the winestems set slightly apart
until the toast is given and the thirst is driven
from us in a wave of warmth made effervescent
by sacred words spoken between the press of life.

the pale of your breasts

like porcelain, crafted by the potter goddess, Freya,
who pours out our hearts into the shells she shapes.
I was bold to dare to touch them, bold to dare to take
them in my hands and kiss them with all the honest ardor
I could summon to convince you of my fealty and love.

eyes of stained glass and fire

There is a point in the arc of living lives parallel
where all the gifts of heaven and thoughts of hell
will not produce an image of provable clarity.
The charity of our prayers, visions taken alive
to be slowly cut down in the tortures we strive
to justify in meandering memories and prophecy.
Buying the worldview of others, sold in paper weighed
by scales that are irrelevant to truth. Parts played
on a stage we are forced upon, acting and reacting
to the directions out of confusion, the cool breeze
of our self-awareness blocked by the windbreak trees
we fooled ourselves into thinking as a clever thing,
to throw in the face of others. Ancient harmonies
reborn in an instant of illumination and honest desire
when one finally looks through eyes of stained glass and fire.

The wind out of Valhalla

Premonitions scattered like coals spun from a burning dervish.
The signs and sigils of fallen dreams, dead and decaying, a lost
commodity. A cost of purity. A purpose mocked. Again. The cult
of cruelty flowing out of weakness, not strength, as we at length
learn the price of our illusions. I have made my peace with life
and will find another road, another place, another purpose fitting
to one compelled to carry the cord wood of the fires of judgements
not rendered anywhere but inside. Pride that lied. Facades fading
into masquerading demons that laugh and run as my first footfall
of a new day echoes on empty silk. The milk of memory stains
the walls of the halls where once stood the sons of man and God
together with the daughters of dreams breathed to sentience
in a pittance of sacrifice on shoulders so broad I marvel you rise
every day to face the blistering mirrors of self-judgement. But
I am not your messiah, I am merely a man. And, on knife point,
proven all too human, all too ready to burn for your love. And
the music nears the silent chorus of the dance of the dream.

Dram

the smallest unit.
beauty and terror
in trace amounts....
it counts for little to our senses.
but its impact is immeasurable,
for it is undetectable and thus
gets past our guards.
shards of the fractured crystal heart
of a forgotten dragon.
flechettes that forget nothing
for they are soulless,
like so many lovers.
but I have seen your fire.
even banked, it burns on...
and I will warm myself oneday
when amotations are again allowed
in the dreams of the waking dead.
until then,
let us drink our drinks of trace elements.
and I will teach you alchemy of the heart.

Damascus, Movement 3

aphrodite
does not barter her beauty
for hollow promise.
wisdom girds glib eloquences in a veil of truth,
the sooth that soothes us
like the blood of aloe fresh cut from a garden
where we swore we would never walk again.
jasmine.
a thought slides like electric lovers
across a sea of tranquility
where the dust is kicked skyward
by the blue flames and boots of the explorers.
I awaken from the dream.
sightless.
paralyzed.
the cold catalepsy illustrating the fear of death
I had forgotten.
but there is an incandescence in the darkness.
and, for once, I sink back to sleep,
aware of God.
and cognizant of the pattern in the tapestry
as I await Rome.
content that Damascus was no illusion
this time.

sparks, like frozen lemons

caught at first glance.
a chance attraction
like a wanderer between stars
caught in the gravity well
of your incandescent eyes.

a sweet smell that draws me in,
seven powers invoked to choke
my last struggles.
a vanity to guard a sanity long lost.
the cost of a vagabond heart.

sparks struck. the kindling catches.
and it matches the fire sweeping
across the dry grass of a solitary soul.
fed by the wind of dreams returning
like the dragons on the horizon.

from out of the city

From out of the city came words. Small words.
Words like lead pellets, ringing on armour, stinging on flesh
and carrying a message of rage and honor defended.

The prophet spoke in broken syntax, the facts spoke
for themselves in time and he was carried to the city square
to be stoned to death, in accordance with the law.

Morning slid over the horizon as if on rails invisible,
and split the night like Trinity. Infinity seemed possible
except for the silence of the waking world, one eye open.

Mourn the night and rise. Rise to your feet and climb
the hill you always said you'd climb before the end of all things.
For it is upon you, even in the optimism of dawn.

Mourn the night and rise. Rise to your vision, rise!
The afterlife is not waiting for you, but you for it,
and the madness of martyrs may call it too soon.

Mourn the night and rise. Spread your bastard wings
and catch the feral winds that come on the sun's fire
to sweep away the night into small shadow piles in corners.

From out of the city came words. Final words.
Words like Eden. Gethsemane. Golgotha. And then.
And then. And then, the silence. The violence of indifference.

Terms of surrender

I can't pretend her love is unconditional.
or even original.
like a sin of omission.
someone left that off before.
and the more
all the more I try to make a cube
of the six coloured squares
and the innocent stares,
the more I get a hypercube.
time running like blood
between ritual fingers
raised in defense
a moment after the arrow
strikes home.
and the stone
anchors the swimmer
to his fate.
there is not grace in victory.
for the acid etching are not sweet.
not even bitter as they burn
a channel
as they churn the curdled cream
of a dream
left too long in the sun.
while you run
for the shadows.

Twice as hot

the fire that burns twice as hot
usually
(note the word)
usually
only burns for half the time.
but if you dare
to take it up a notch
to where gas becomes
nuclear plasma
and the oxidation
becomes fusion
it can last forever.
it is just few have
the courage
to burn so hot
that they blind
the world and
risk annihilating
the universe
with their glory.
for we are mortals and
immortality
frightens us.
so I will wait
in the torus
and see if you show.
for I saw the spark
in your eyes
as you raised your head
and dropped your guard
and held me
in a doorway
in New York.

the common tongue

the orthography of poets
belongs in poetry.
not in words spoken
in pain or anger or fear
of losing something or someone
held so dear
that you feel death upon you.
that is a time for the babysteps
of simple words, where commonality
is more likely true. a basic
tongue where truths are not
garbled amid the noise of well meaning
friends who read letters like
Rorschach tests and listened that night
you raved until late, finding hate
in wounded love and bitter tears.

undefined

I remember how you wept
when I spoke the words
to you. undefined
the role you would play.
it made you walk to the fence
and ask for a dictionary
that you might ferry your heart
to a safe place. an embrace
between lovers destined
and damned. I am here now,
at the fence you built.
where sits the Raven.
and you left a note for me.
"major, yet undefined"
cryptic words before a dance.
deadly words the morning after.
the mourning after.

Lovers at the well

kisses like candy set in handcut wooden bowls.
torches unlit to hide in the darkness, stolen
embraces. traces of love. faces touching
the wind. once skinned knees, now merged
souls. children to maturity, purity of passion
by the well where they played not so long
ago, pretending to find fascination in the stones
the peddler kicked while calling out his wares.
copper knives and wooden bowls. mixing mischief.

kisses

I miss your kiss
and want it back.

the panther on the beach

A poet's dream and invocation of dark divinity
spun of the ethereal webs of chance and sweet mortality.
A future memory calling of the panther on the beach.
Forbidden and forever. The rose, she grows just out of reach,
representing a resonant sweetness, nectar of a peach,
a poet's dream and invocation of dark divinity.
So innocently the Judas goat, la belle dame sans merci.
My blood, it burns in cascade turns, now in bondage to be free:
a future memory calling of the panther on the beach.
Hardwired, soul to sinew, as if the vengeful prophets preach
a fallen grace of lost face, disremembering what we teach.
A poet's dream and invocation of dark divinity.
I gaze, in rapt amazement, committing all to memory,
raging in a cage called propriety. A false dignity.
A future memory calling of the panther on the beach.
A visit to the edge of the enamored infinity.
Woven in words incarnate and the elegance of my speech.
A poet's dream and invocation of dark divinity.
A future memory calling of the panther on the beach.

Night of a thousand colours

crisp, cold and calculating.
the proper pronouncements
on tongues cut from leather
birthed in a sea of tranquility
and madness.
the blossom on a daffodil
crushed, a poet's hushed
prayers. and stairs that
ascend a tower, friend
to the night of a thousand colours.
duller than plain song.
duller than a white
plastic knife, serrated
ridges worn off on the
edge of the picnic table
where we spread a feast...
halfway down the road
to the farthest ocean.
another catalog case
of illusions and fantasies
to sit on a shelf forever,
like a lost clay wizard, forever
wondering of his exile from
his brother. another time.
another place. another face
and another crime. red
as lips in shy surrender.
indigo as the night.
hallucinations.
benedictions.
and sacred vows.
turning sanctuary
into a prison and
survival into
slow
lingering
wasted
death.

but my breath
will not be wasted.
and colours tasted
never forgotten
as long as I have words
and the will to use them.

The Reich of self-discipline

you are alone because you choose to be alone.
I am alone because you choose to be alone.
the balance is not there, but the justice is.
truth like a peach,
crimson with overripeness,
nectar oozing in rivulets of pink sweetness
not unlike the last feast of passion I will ever taste.
memories unerased by the passage of time,
the message of crime uncommitted.
unremitting love.
sad.
as sad as a clock's song of solace.
less than the truth, more than a lie.
we cry in corners hidden from the watchful eyes
of our internal, eternal, infernal critic.
epic and poetic epigrams that slam doors
of opportunity as the fruit
slowly
slides
from its anchorage and
falls.
falls.
falls from the summit of dark kisses
and the joy of love play
into the isolation of the hard earth
amid the bitter blades of sawgrass
and the Reich of self-discipline.

in the arms of the dragon

I kiss the beauty of your complexities.
your scars are a familiar terrain
to my lips, cut as they have been
a thousand times for greater
and lesser crimes unpenanced.
I do not doubt your beauty
and in the arms of the dragon
you fit like a gem in the forehead
of a smiling Buddha, alive and dreaming
of new winds yet to blow and yet
you seem to know where, if not when
they will take you, make you
all that you are already in the arms of the Dragon.

The faceted sphere: 28

an etching of an unlikely and improbable and
impossible embrace that is cut into a warm
and plastic mind in honest desire. gentle
and unmocking this imagined unlocking
of the vaults of pleasure in a reality so far from here
that only infinite eyes can pierce the mists of distance and logic.
a puzzle to be prodded as I chase the chaste illusions
of a vision spawned in a single mental image of paradise
consumed for the want of a pauper's measure
of passion and sincere devotion. a whisper
raising fierce illusions of a chance to teach the dance
to an earnest paramour, the price of immortality
the only currency of worth to offer.

William F. DeVault

Cassiopeia's garden: wildflowers

fistfuls of colour
to give to my mother
to show her I love her

pride of authorship

we pride ourselves on our creations.
and yet, our greatest work lays
obscured by all our work-room
clutter emotions. sawdust and
that lost hammer, thrown in a
corner, not out of disrespect,
but haste and auteur's passion.
this script is grander than any comedy.
this poem is sweeter than any cycle.
this evocation advertises the best
in woman and in man, better than any
brochure or slogan. we are the art
and will be judged one day in
the eyes and minds and hearts
of those who descend from our
actions and our fleshes, based
on our pride of authorship.

a summoned fire

claim for me your tattered soul
that leads your form to wander, soft,
on bare feet to the window's light
(to shroud your curves in barest light)
that I should send dark prayers aloft
to be with you, and play a role,
of conquered and the conqueror:
the paramour you can't forget,
who brought his heart without remorse
to walk your life like challenged course,
and share with you, without regret,
a passion damned forevermore.
allow me all that I desire
and I will share a summoned fire.

About the author

William F. DeVault is the author of thousands of poems and several books, including **The Compleat Panther Cycles** and **Love Gods of a Forgotten Religion**.

Born in Greenville, South Carolina, he counts Los Angeles his home, despite being named by the Appalachian Educational Initiative as one of 50 Outstanding Creative Artists educated in West Virginia.

The poet gratefully acknowledges the work of Mariya Andriichuk, who serves as both model and photographer for the cover of this volume, See more of her work at http://www.ladymartist.com.

CPSIA information can be obtained at www.ICGtesting.com
Printed in the USA
BVOW011136230613

324067BV00015B/309/P

9 781478 176763